# EPISODE 8

"COFFEE IS A LANGUAGE IN ITSELF."
- JACKIE CHAN

Caffeine, whether you use it or misuse it, you're probably leaving the benefits of one of the most powerful tools for peak performance on the table. So let's teach you the science: how to use caffeine for elevated cognitive performance.

Now, caffeine has shaped the growth and direction of civilization over the last 3,000 years. Ever wondered what your city skyline would look like if caffeine never existed?

Although steel and glass giant buildings built on a foundation of caffeinated consciousness, you see, caffeine is the molecule powering the productivity behind the Enlightenment, the Industrial Revolution, and the IT Revolution.
And I think you could argue that caffeine is one of the uncredited co-creators of the civilization that we live in.

So, how do we harness caffeine to maximize its upside without the downside? The solution is in the caffeine Commandments, which we're going to cover in a moment. But in order to understand why these caffeine Commandments work so well, we need to look at the science. And before we look at the science, let's start with helping you determine your caffeine archetype.

Which is the first step in attaining caffeine mastery.

So, which of these four archetypes resonates most? First off, we've got the reformed. This is you if you once relied on caffeine heavily but now you've quit completely. You've felt the burn and then decided you've had enough.

Second, we've got the skeptics. You may think caffeine is harmful or unhealthy, will give you unbalanced energy, or negatively affect your sleep. Or you don't like the idea of relying on external sources of energy, so you don't use caffeine at all.

Then, third, we have the unmindful users. You use caffeine but without much thought or intention. Often, you overdo it. You're not really sure if it's harming you, but you definitely know that you're not using it optimally.

And then there's a very small chance you're in the fourth category: the mindful master, where you use caffeine to propel you forward into deep focus and long uninterrupted states of flow and peak performance. The true problem isn't that caffeine is just bad; that you need to quit it. So, you need to avoid it. Rather, given its impact and potency, a better question to start with is: how can I use caffeine in a way that serves my productivity, aids my health, and drives me into Flow State with reliability?

Now, back to the science for a second.
New research suggests that caffeine can actually trigger a flow State. Now, flow is an optimal State of Consciousness where we feel our best and we perform our best. But for many professionals, Flow State, though incredibly useful, is equally elusive.

So, can caffeine really trigger this elusive State? Well, in this research, we have found strong correlations between caffeine and the onset of Flow State. First, caffeine stimulates increased dopamine and norepinephrine, which drive attention into the present moment and help catalyze flow. Flow follows focus, caffeine heightens focus.

What it also does is stimulate the release of cortisol and epinephrine, the fight-or-flight hormone, which prepares the body for intense exertion, gearing you up for flow and prolonging the Flow State.

Third, caffeine desensitizes adenosine A1 receptors in the brain, which allows dopamine to have a greater effect, which means you get more focus more easily and then more flow off the back end of that focus.

The research makes clear that it's a shame to not use caffeine or to misuse caffeine because it is a profound lever on peak cognitive performance. So with that, let's have you attain caffeine Mastery and master the caffeine Commandments for flow, of which there are six.

# 1. "THOU SHALT CONDITION YOURSELF FOR FLOW WITH CAFFEINE TO TRIGGER FLOW"

Oh, with caffeine, we want to use something called classical conditioning. Now, classical conditioning is about learning through association. A Russian psychologist, Ivan Pavlov, noticed that his dogs salivated when they saw food, and then he rang a bell when giving them that food.

Eventually, just ringing the bell made the dog salivate as they'd associated the bell with the food, even when the food wasn't present. And we can do a similar thing with caffeine and flow. You can use caffeine as a stimulus, and engaging in challenging work as the response that we're trying to condition.

So over time, caffeine becomes a trigger signaling to the brain that it's time to enter a state of deep focus. But the combination of caffeine and flow makes classical conditioning more effective for two reasons.

The first is that caffeine provides an altered state of consciousness. Caffeine is a drug. It alters how we feel, it alters the way we think and see the world when we are caffeinated.

Flow does the same thing. Flow is also an altered or non-ordinary state of consciousness, and research shows that when either the stimulus or the response alters your state of consciousness, it makes the conditioning effect tighter.

But when both of these things (in this case, caffeine and flow) provide an altered state of consciousness, the conditioning and association between those two variables becomes even tighter.

So when you sit down for your first big flow block of the day, that three-hour block or 90-minute block, whatever it is, where you're going to tackle a meaty high-priority, high-leverage task, that's when you want to hit the caffeine and watch as it'll start to drive you into flow more and more over time.

So flow is just one part of a four-phase cycle, beginning with struggle and leading to the release of the Flow State itself, and then the recovery phase on the back end. In the struggle phase of the flow cycle, the brain has to load all of the new information it's receiving about the task it's engaging with. It involves norepinephrine and cortisol release, high prefrontal cortex activity. Lots going on up here in the front of the brain and increased cognitive load.

It's hard, it's a struggle At the onset of a task like this, the key is, though caffeine can shortcut the struggle phase, boosting us through it by increasing alertness. Caffeine reduces cognitive load and makes information processing more efficient.

It also boosts dopamine, which gives you more focus without you having to fight for every ounce of that focus and exert as much conscious effort. This moves you to the release phase of the flow cycle, which is characterized by relaxation and letting go of conscious control around the task, loosening our grip so to speak.

And this allows faster and more fluid cognition. Catego, so use caffeine to boost yourself through the struggle phase, shortcut and struggle down, moving faster into release, and then of course, faster into the Flow State itself.

# 3. "THOU SHALT TIME YOUR CAFFEINE INTAKE."

You may know this one. So, Dr. Andrew Hubman, an incredible staff from neuroscientists you've probably heard of, has done a great job educating the world about caffeine and cortisol, the wake-up hormone our body naturally cranks out for us first thing in the morning to elevate alertness.

If you ingest caffeine too early upon waking, it crowds your adenosine receptors, causing the cortisol to compete with the caffeine, which leads to a mid-morning crash.

If you leave the adenosine receptors unoccupied, open for business for the cortisol for a little bit, you'll naturally wake up and be more alert in the morning with cortisol rather than caffeine. So the rule is cortisol first, caffeine second, and you want to wait about 30 minutes after waking up before you consume caffeine.

Now, technically, based on the research Huberman psyched, it is longer than that, but for practical purposes, many people can't wait that much longer just due to the nature of their morning and how their day goes. So, leave at least 30 minutes. A little bit longer is better, but at least 30 minutes. That's how you time caffeine for the front end of the day.

Then, on the back end of the day, be careful of caffeine Half-Life. Avoid consuming caffeine at least 10 hours before bed, otherwise, it will interfere with sleep. That means if you go to bed at 10 pm, have your last dose of caffeine by 12 pm. Remember, no amount of caffeine can compare to the performance-enhancing benefits of a single night of sound sleep.

Your sleep is the base; caffeine is something that you can use to dial up the natural and organic cognitive performance that you get by sleeping well. Consuming caffeine when well-rested is also just an incredible euphoric experience.

We want to sleep well, and we do not want caffeine to compromise sleep at all. So, 10 hours before you go to bed is your last dose of caffeine.

# 4. "THOU SHALT CALIBRATE THE DOSE."

The dose makes the poison. Too little caffeine, you won't feel the effects or fatigue will be even exacerbated. Too much caffeine, well, you know what that feels like.

The Jitters are not fun, the Jitters are not pretty. So we don't want that. To keep it simple, start with about 100 milligrams a day of caffeine, which is just about a regular cup of coffee. Observe how your body responds and adjust accordingly. If it's slightly too much, then just drop it down to half that, see what 50 milligrams is like.
If it's too little, double it. If you can handle even more without it disturbing your sleep or overstimulating your nervous system, you could try a little bit more and go all the way up to 300 milligrams. My friend swears by 40 milligrams, for me, I'm closer to 200 milligrams for my caffeine sweet spot.

The point is, you want to know what dose level is optimal for you in general, and you also want to know what dose level is optimal for you in specific situations, such as when you are fatigued and underslept. And we want to avoid the common mistake of underdosing caffeine when fatigued.

Yes, underdosing caffeine when fatigued. So if you're fatigued, meaning you've gotten, let's say, 30% or less of your normal night's sleep, let's say if you normally sleep nine hours, you've gotten maybe just over six hours. So you know, technically, you're fatigued based on that definition. Well, if so, you're going to want to increase your caffeine dose by about 50%.

Because when you're fatigued, your brain has a high level of adenosine, so you need a higher dose of caffeine to counteract it. That means if you normally have one cup of coffee, have a cup and a half. If you normally have two, have three cups when fatigued. And this does not want to become a pattern. We do not want to use caffeine as a Band-Aid to cover up for fatigue.

"This is for usage in the rare instances when we just can't get around it, and we're underslept now. Another quirk regarding caffeine and sleep that's usually not talked about is that, counter-intuitively, if you dose the caffeine just right and expend energy cognitively through flow, caffeine dosing can actually help you sleep better by causing you to time the caffeine dip and decrease of the half-life at the same time that you want to wind down at the end of the day and go to sleep.

This is because you'll get a bigger shift into a down-regulated nervous system, a parasympathetic state, from the sympathetic state the caffeine results in, which can actually help us wind down and help us sleep better. But again, dose and timing are critical for this to be the case.

Now, caffeine commandment number five: "Thou shalt give caffeine companions." Ever notice how sometimes caffeine feels just right? You're alert but not jittery, focused but not wired, and other times it feels off and you're bouncing off the walls, you've got that jagged energy. Well, part of this is dose, but part of this is synergy.

You see, the trick to getting it just right is to dial in the delivery mechanism and mix your caffeine with other substances that aid its absorption and positively impact its effect.

So, coffee doesn't just contain caffeine, it also contains antioxidants. It also contains things like theobromine. Yerba mate contains caffeine, but it also contains polyphenols and a number of other compounds that can help smooth out the caffeine. Then there's good old tea, which the Irish, like myself, are absolutely mad for, and that contains other compounds like l-theanine. And then, of course, you've got energy drinks, which contain bucket loads of other compounds, unfortunately some of them sugar, but also even the diet ones, B vitamins, amino acids like taurine, or herbal extracts like ginseng.

All of these compounds are going to alter the way the caffeine feels.
Caffeine, whether you use it or misuse it, you're probably leaving the benefits of one of the most powerful tools for peak performance on the table.

# HOW TO USE CAFFEINE FOR ELEVATED COGNITIVE PERFORMANCE.

You want to test and see which delivery mechanism tends to suit you best and lend itself to optimal cognitive performance. Now, the general rule of thumb when it comes to caffeine and its companions is to pair it with two things always, and these are l-theanine and H2O or water.

We want to use a two-to-one ratio with both of these. For example, if you take 100 milligrams of caffeine (which is a standard cup of coffee), have 200 milligrams of l-theanine for every cup of coffee, and drink two cups of water. Really simple! Research shows that this combo can help you stay focused without feeling overstimulated.

A lot of people ask me if I had to recommend one thing to get into flow more consistently, what would it be? A cheap hack you can use to really elevate cognitive performance for about a three-hour period is to remain fasted, usually in the morning, and to dose the right amount of caffeine. Let's say 100 milligrams, plus the l-theanine and water. Dive into work undistracted, and you will notice a very significant cognitive effect.

Now, a few months back, I spent a month in Nasara in Costa Rica, one of the most beautiful places on Earth, and I was smashing back the coffees with my favorite barista in the world, Juan. Shout out to Juan!

And one day, I hit my third espresso. I finished it, metabolized it, and then I realized I didn't feel any different to before I had my first one. And that's because I had violated one of the most important caffeine Commandments, which is: "Thou shalt abstain from caffeine sporadically."
You've experienced this for yourself; caffeine sensitivity gradually decreases and you make yourself immune from the drug. So what you need to do is what's technically called a caffeine wash.

Here's a simple rule for it: take at least one day off per week from caffeine entirely. I think Sundays are a really great day for this; it just allows your nervous system to reset. And then, in addition to taking one day a week off, we want to take one full week per quarter off caffeine.

Now, you may be thinking, 'Oh God, that sounds brutal, doing a day a week without it or a week a quarter without it. I need my daily caffeine to function well.' The idea here is not to deprive you of caffeine, but to give you more out of the caffeine that you do use.

Keep yourself hypersensitive to caffeine so that when you have your big Americano in the morning, you can feel it squeezing juice out of those neurons just like you wanted. Now, if you follow these six caffeine Commandments, caffeine will start to become an incredible companion that drops you deep into the zone, and you'll minimize its potential drawbacks.

If you found this book useful, think of a friend or a couple of friends who either misuse caffeine, don't use caffeine, or abuse caffeine. Let's get the message out about how to use caffeine optimally so we can have more caffeinated Consciousness in the world, creating more useful things for the world.

Printed in Great Britain
by Amazon

46360091R00020